I0509459

THIS SPACE COLORING BOOK

BELONGS TO:

____

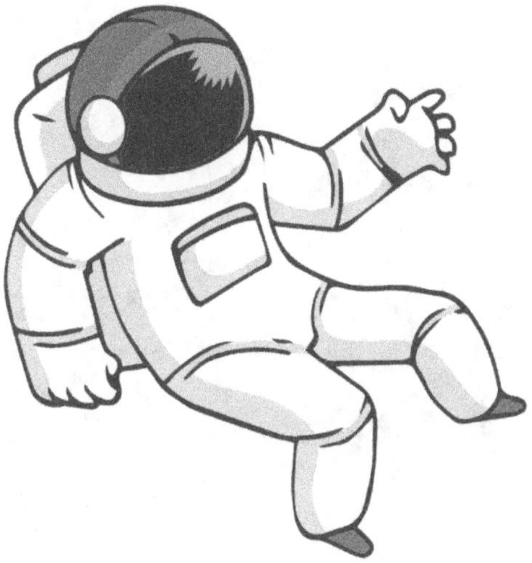

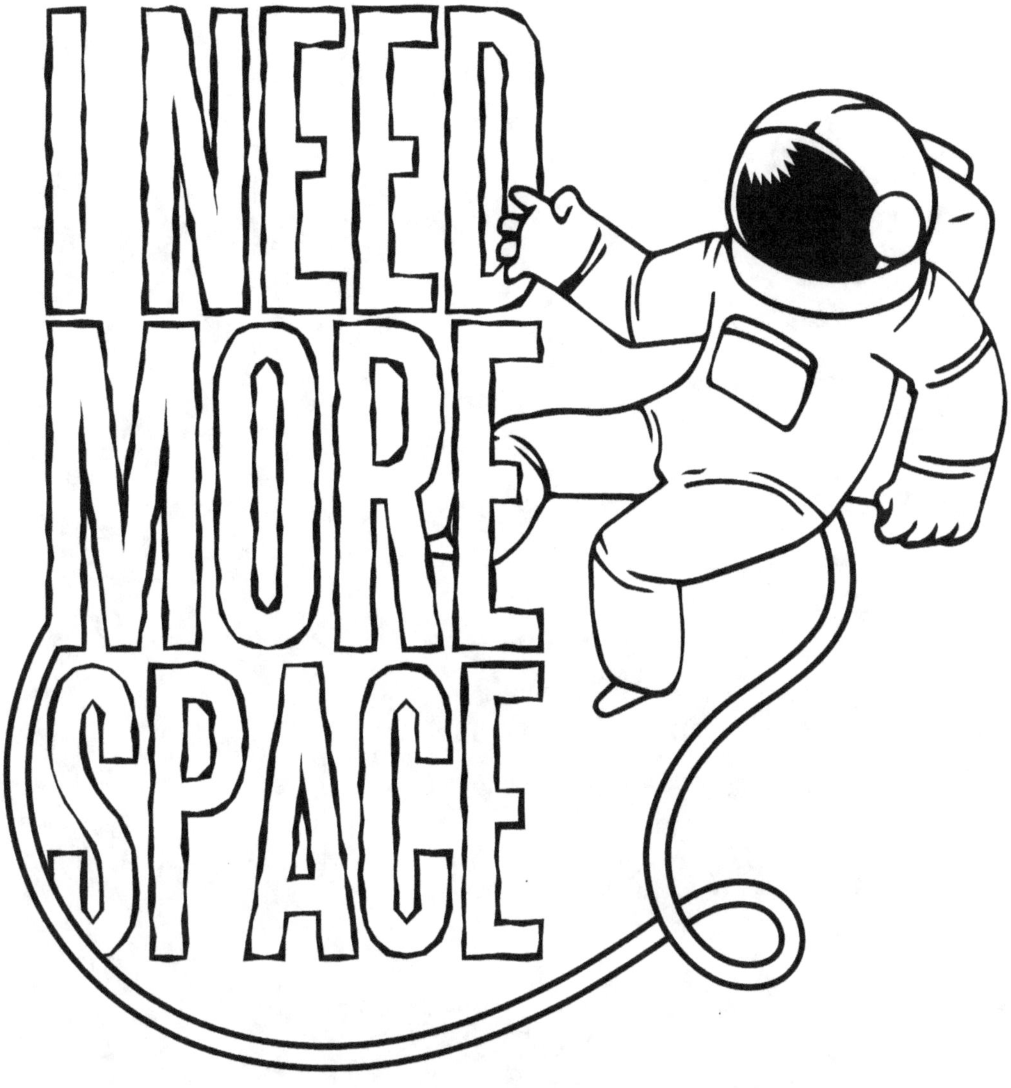
I NEED
MORE
SPACE

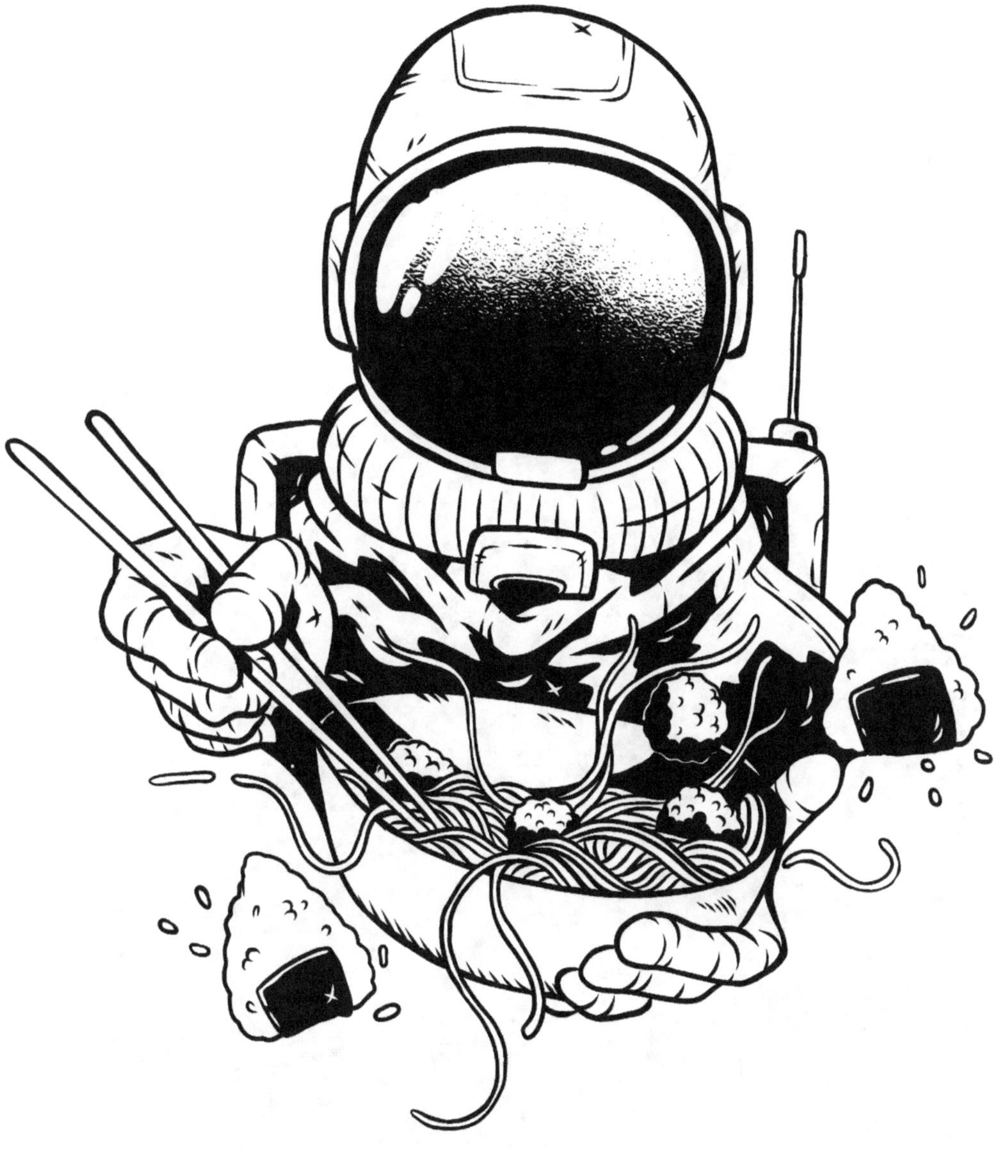

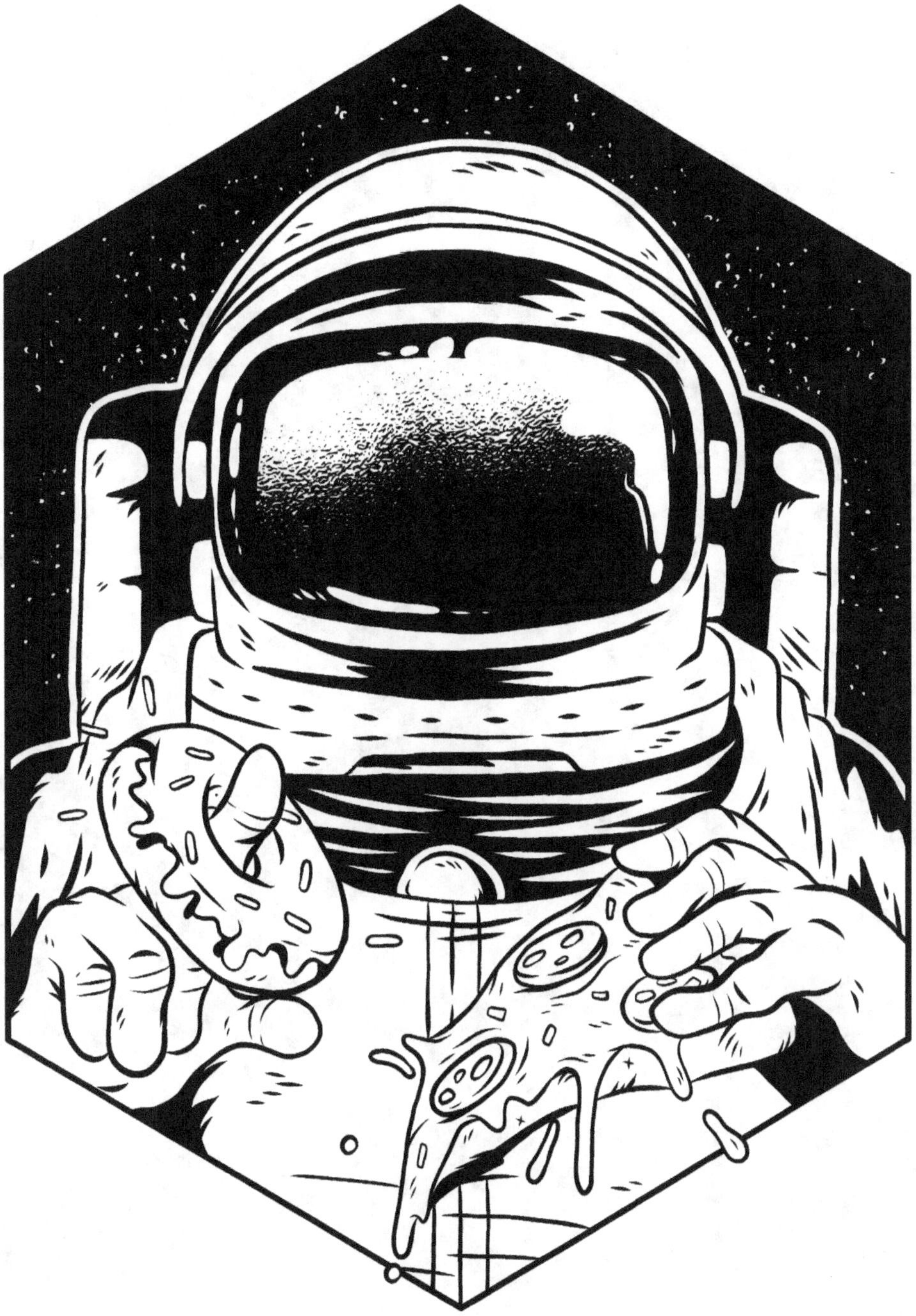

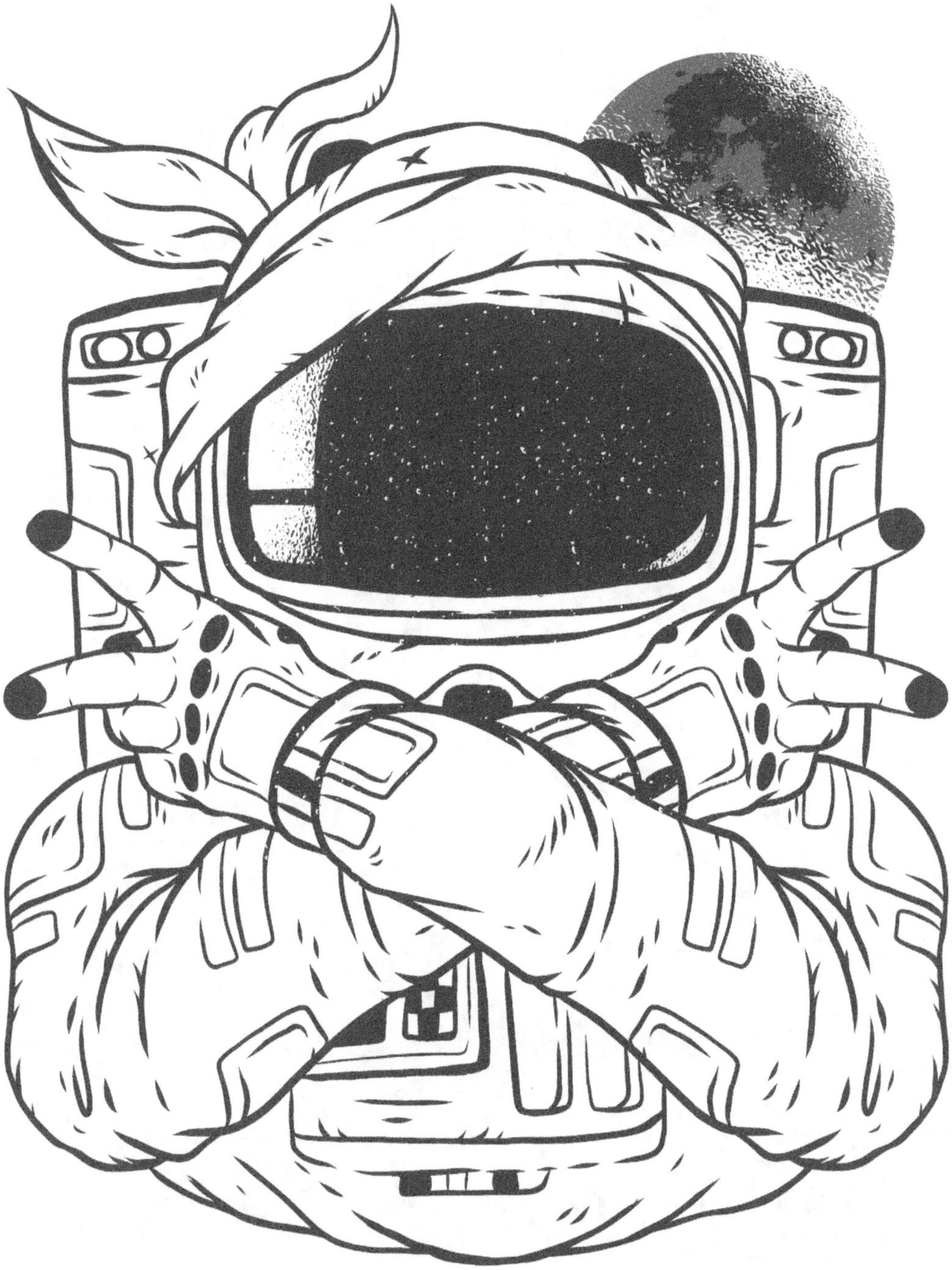

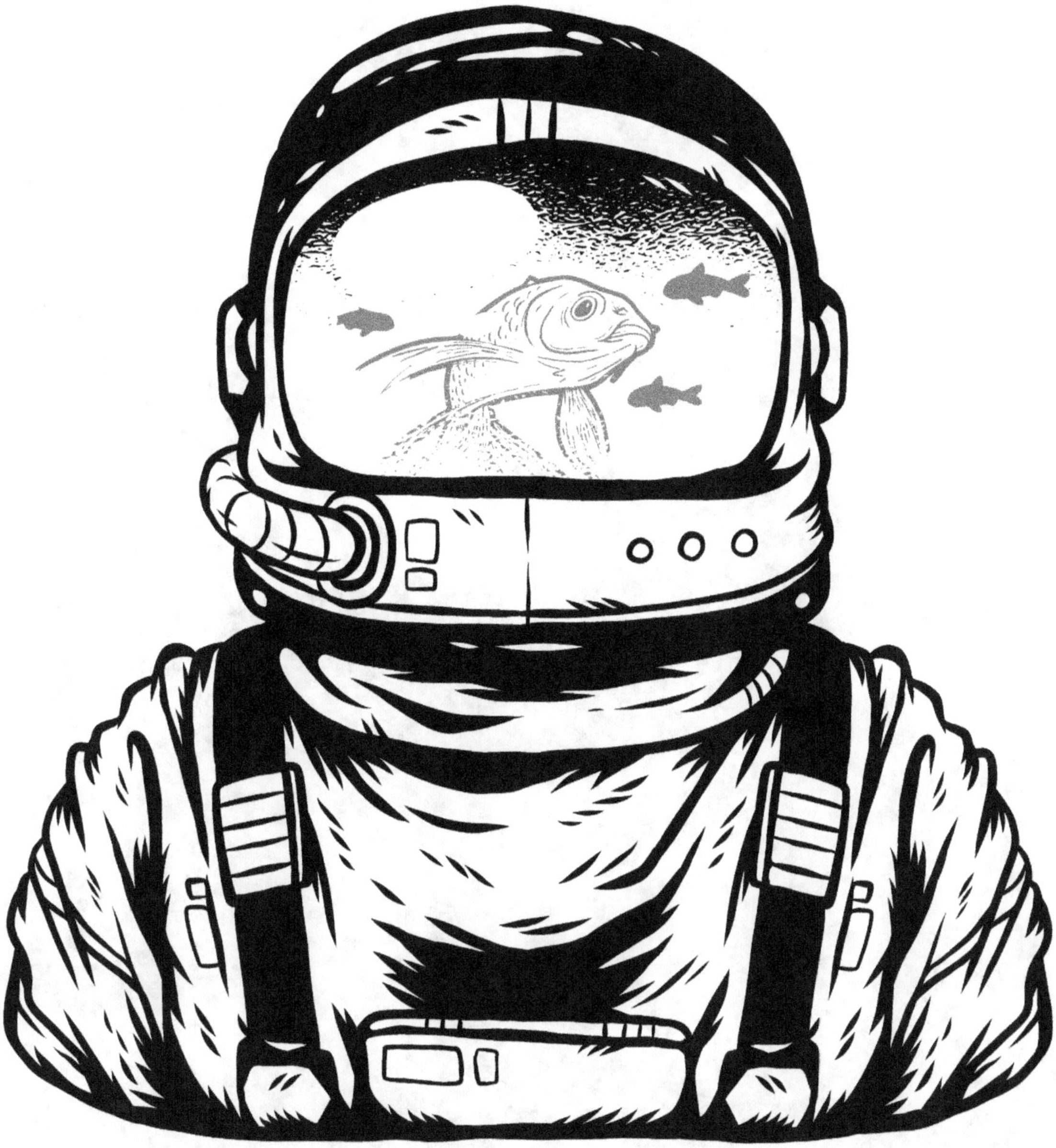

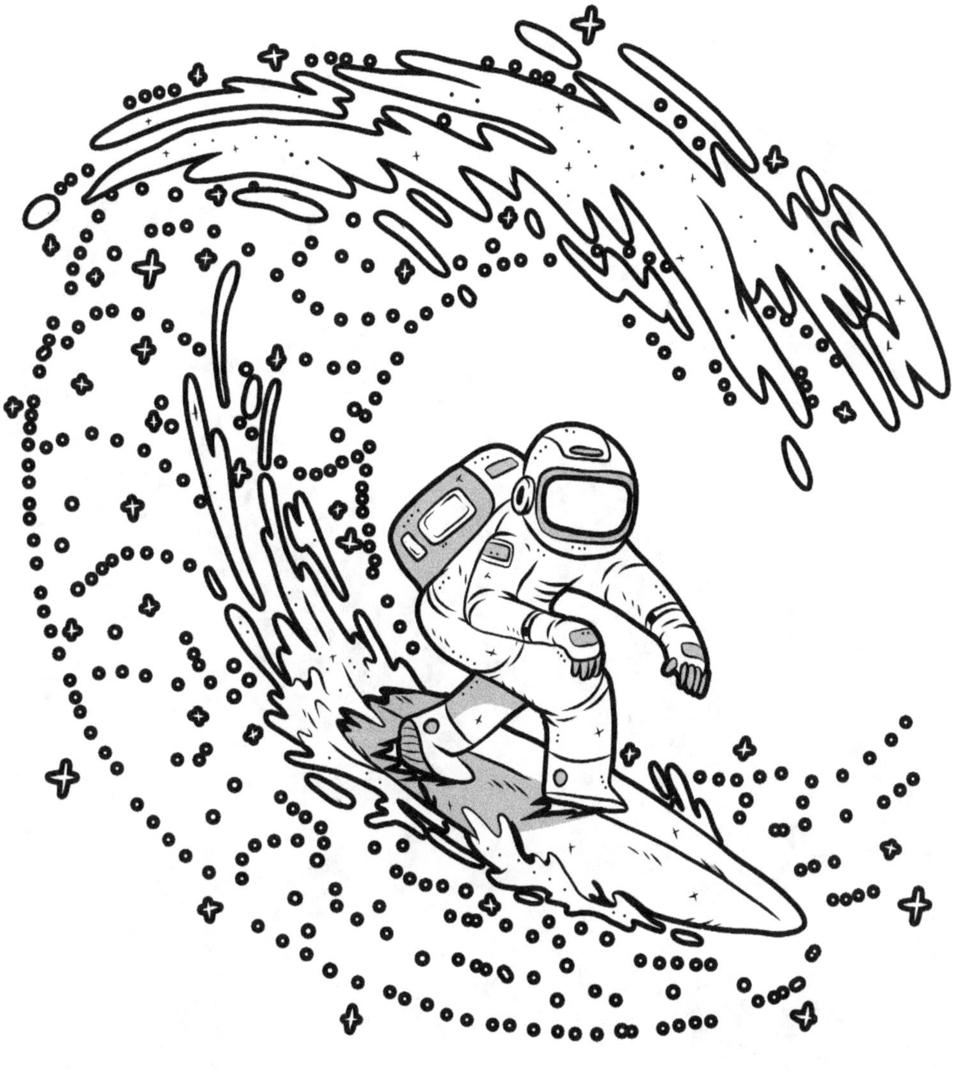

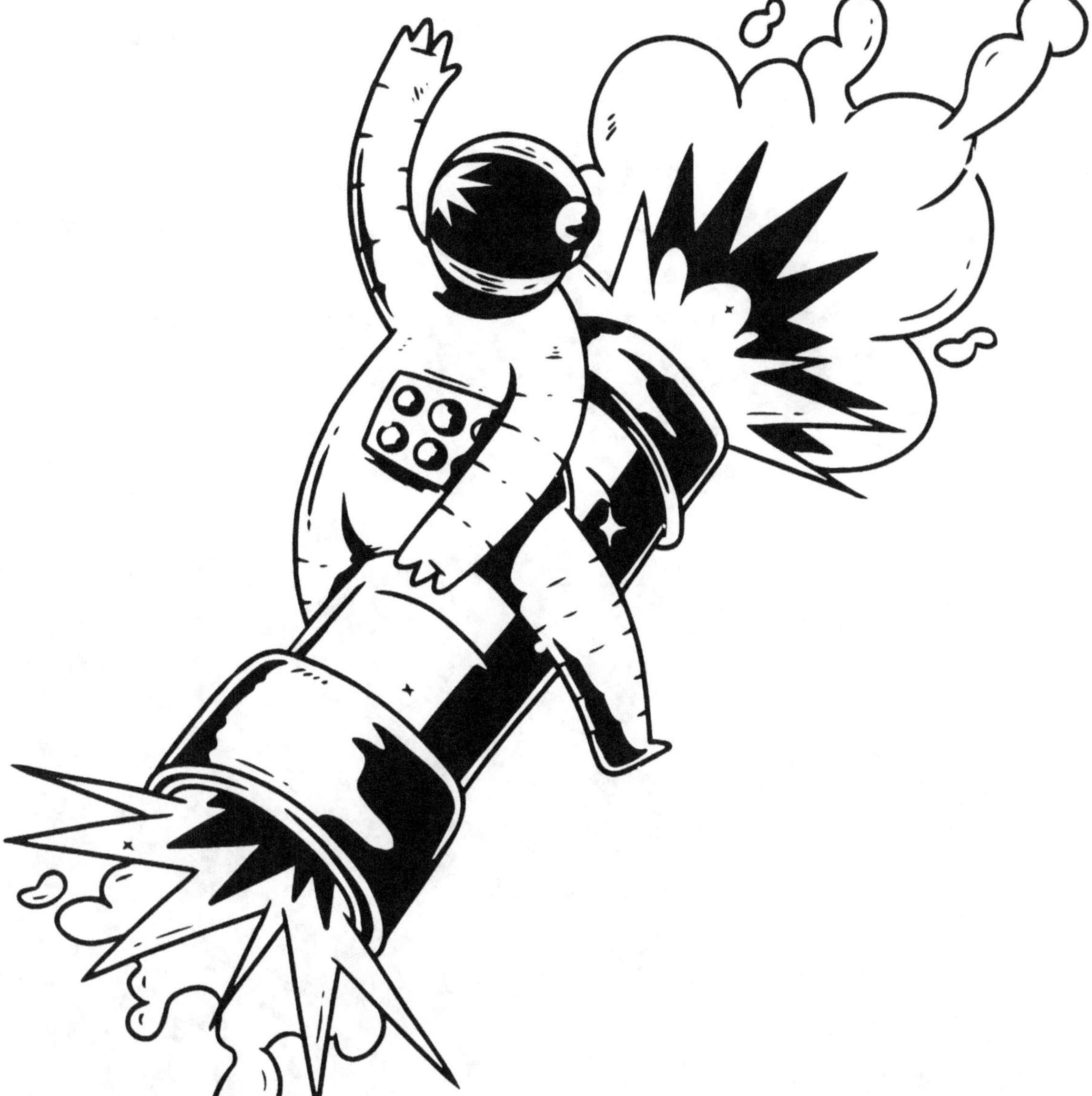

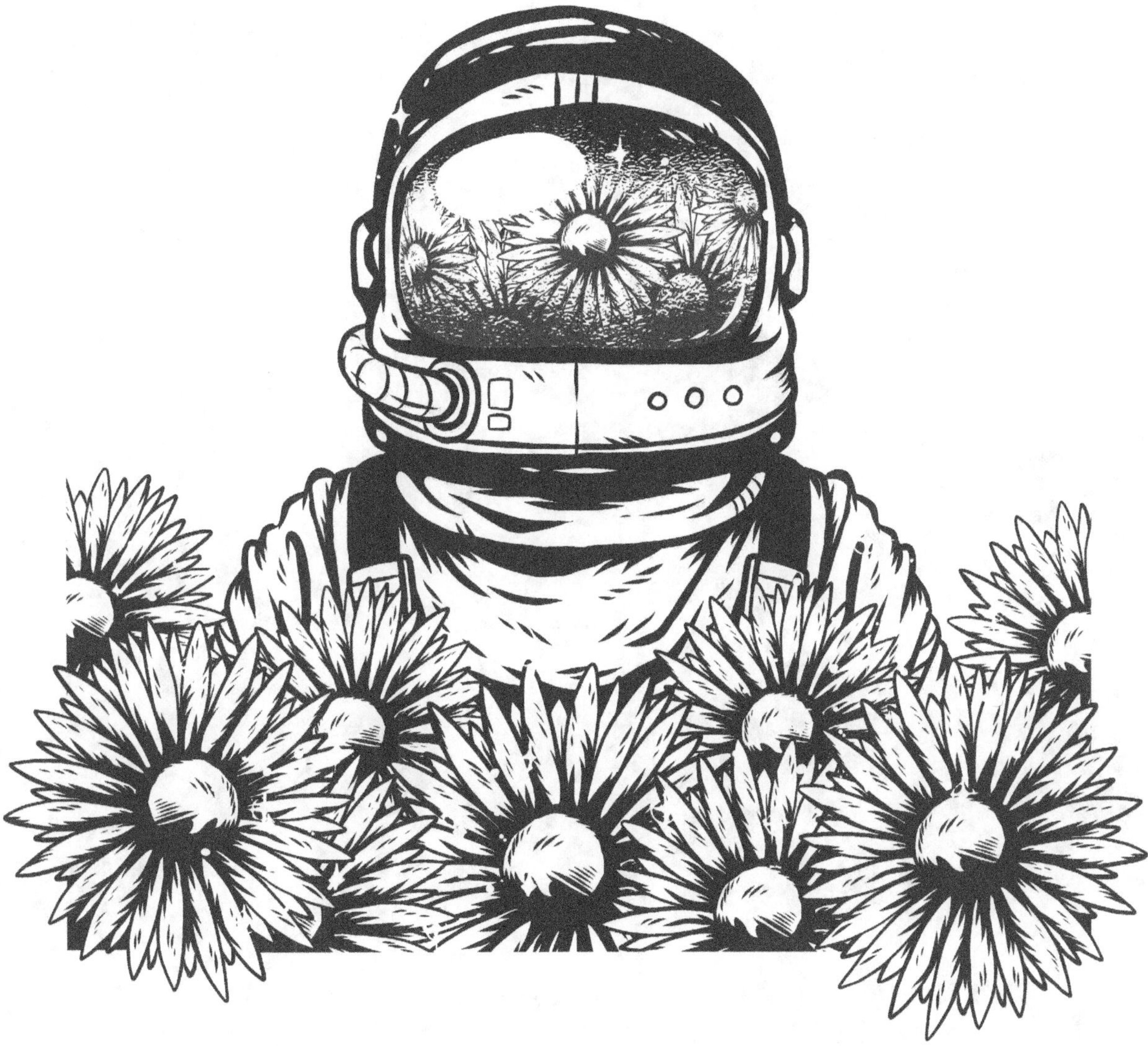

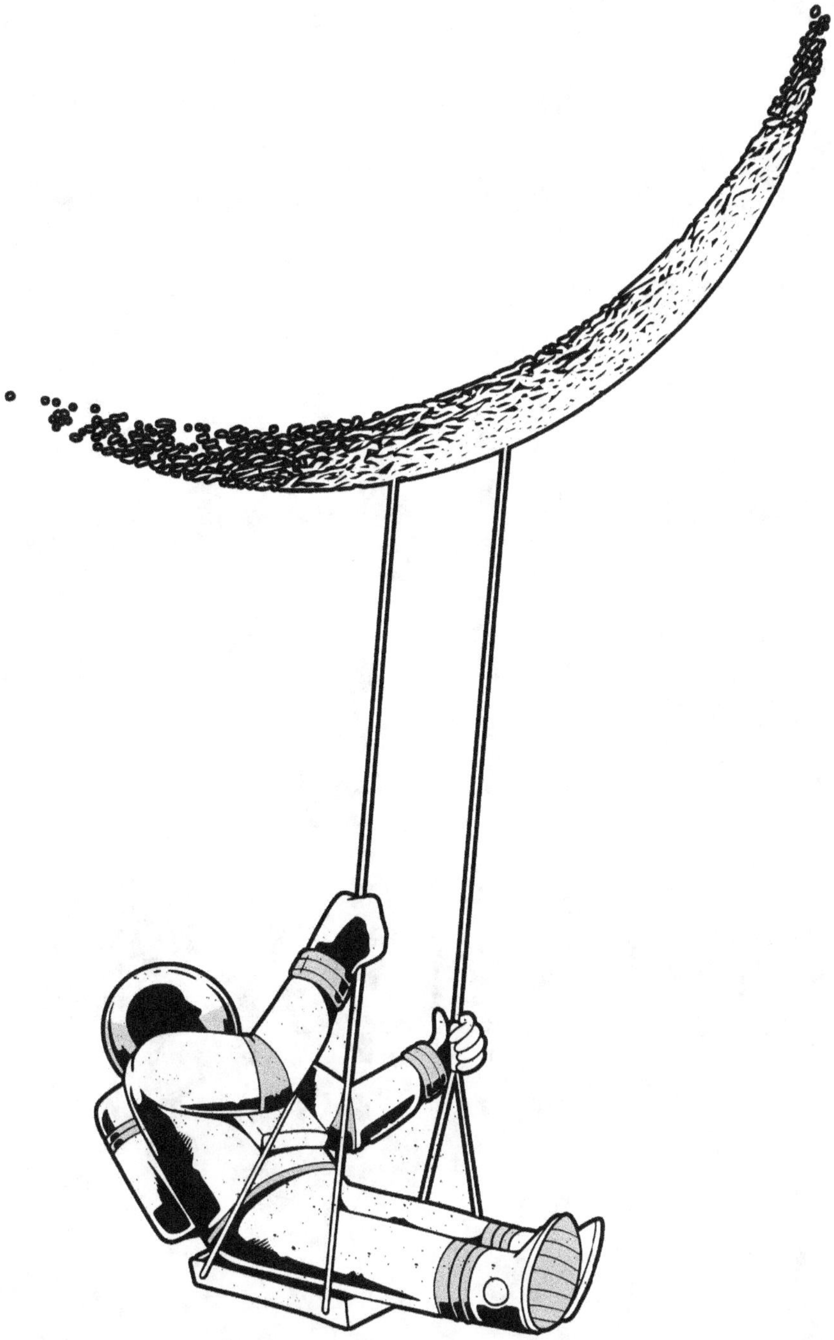

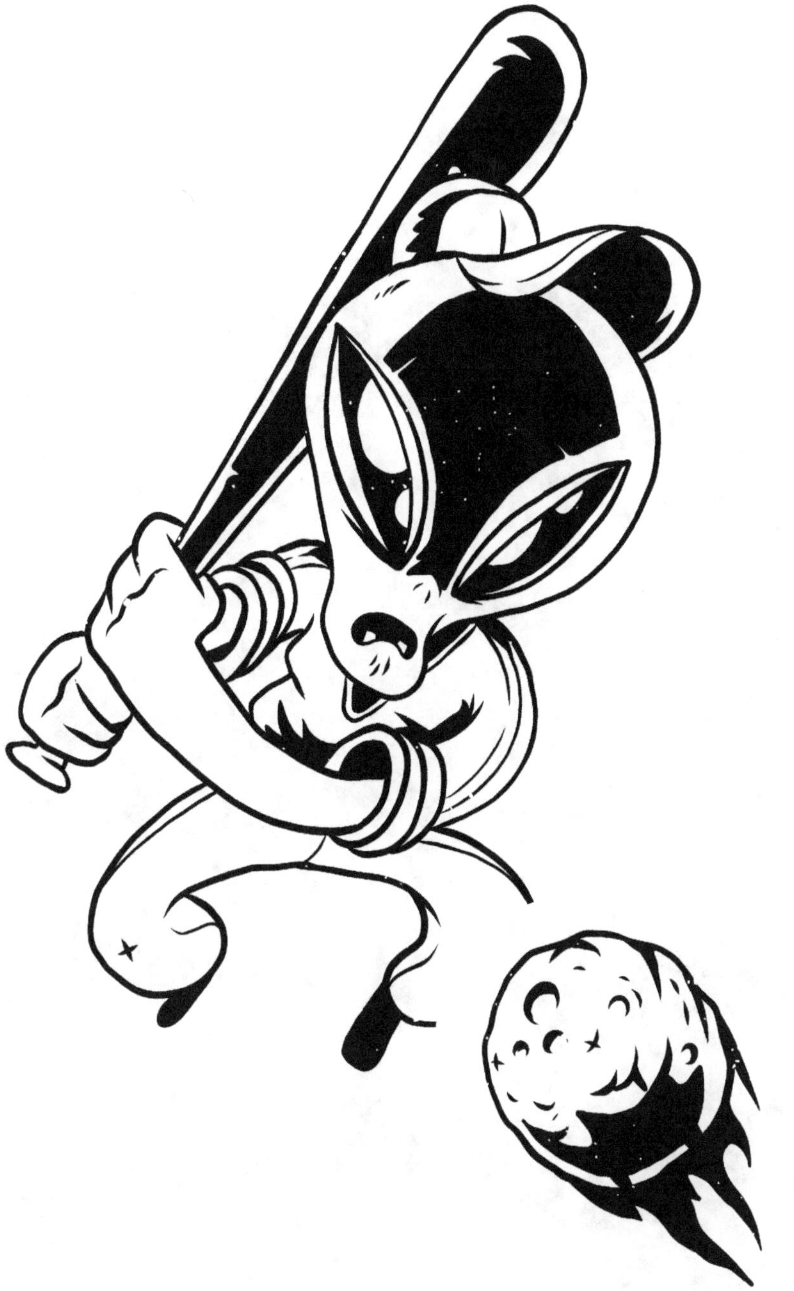

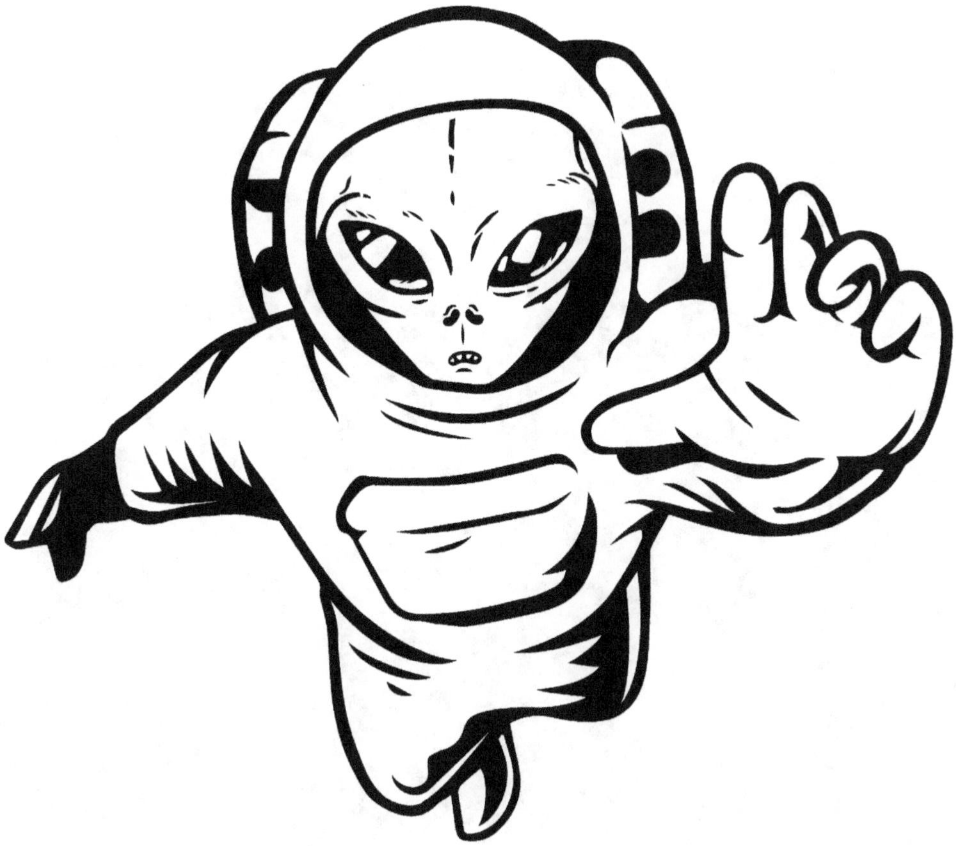

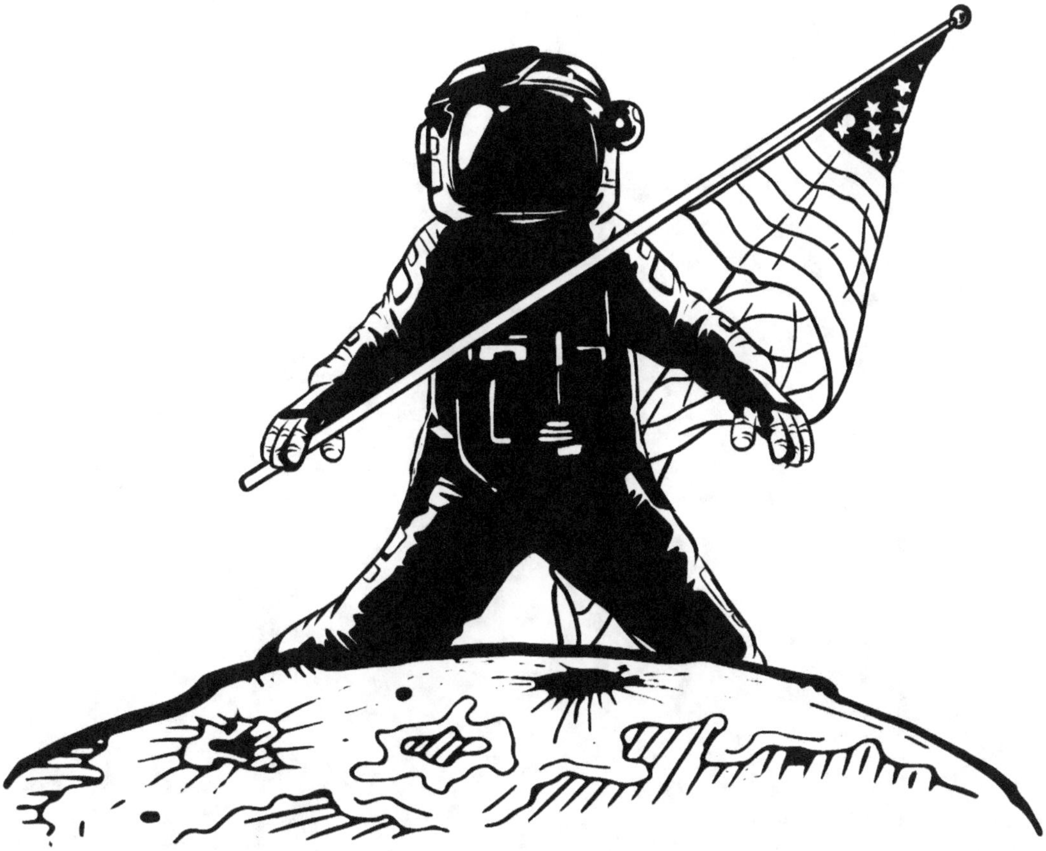

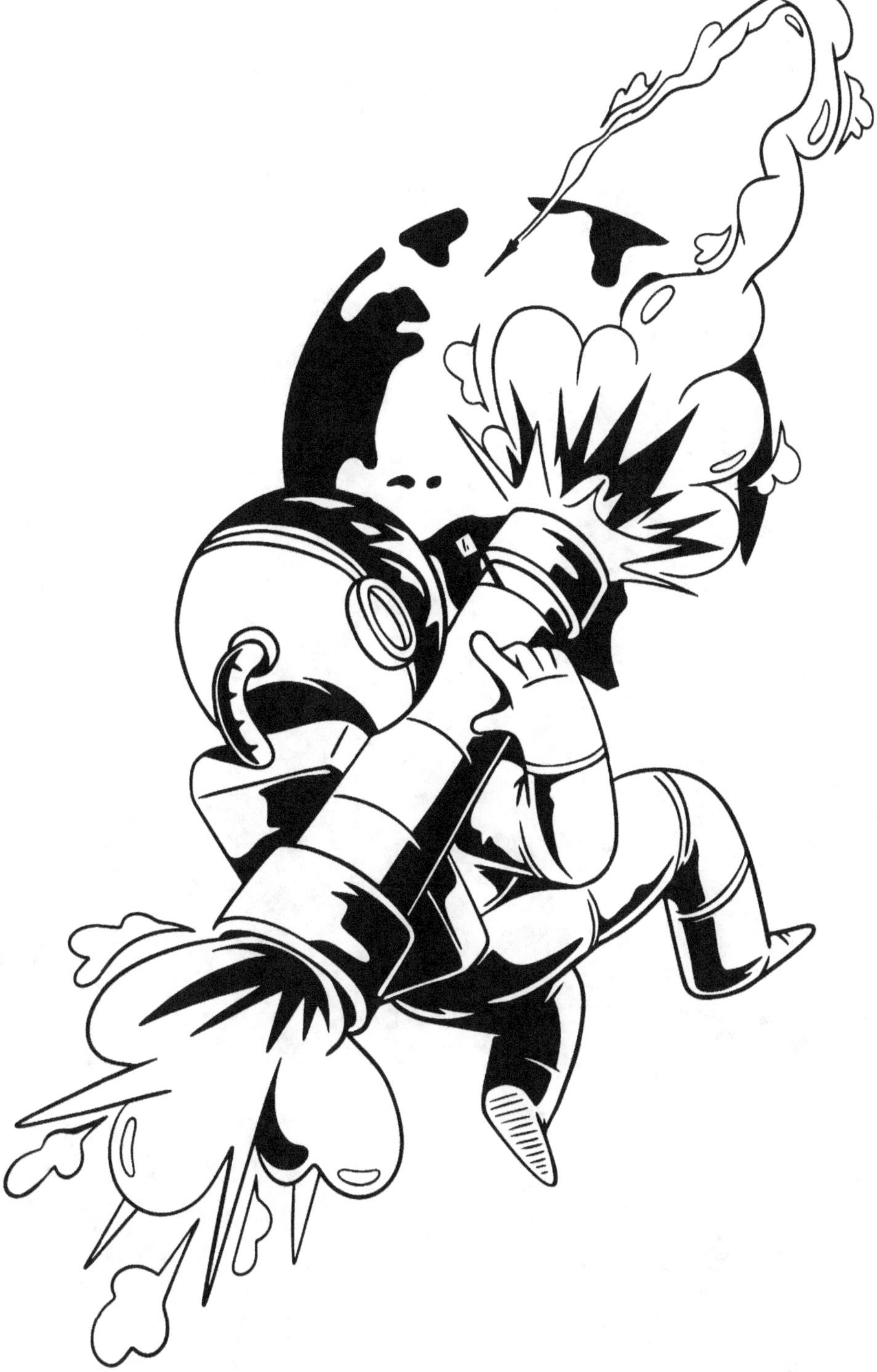

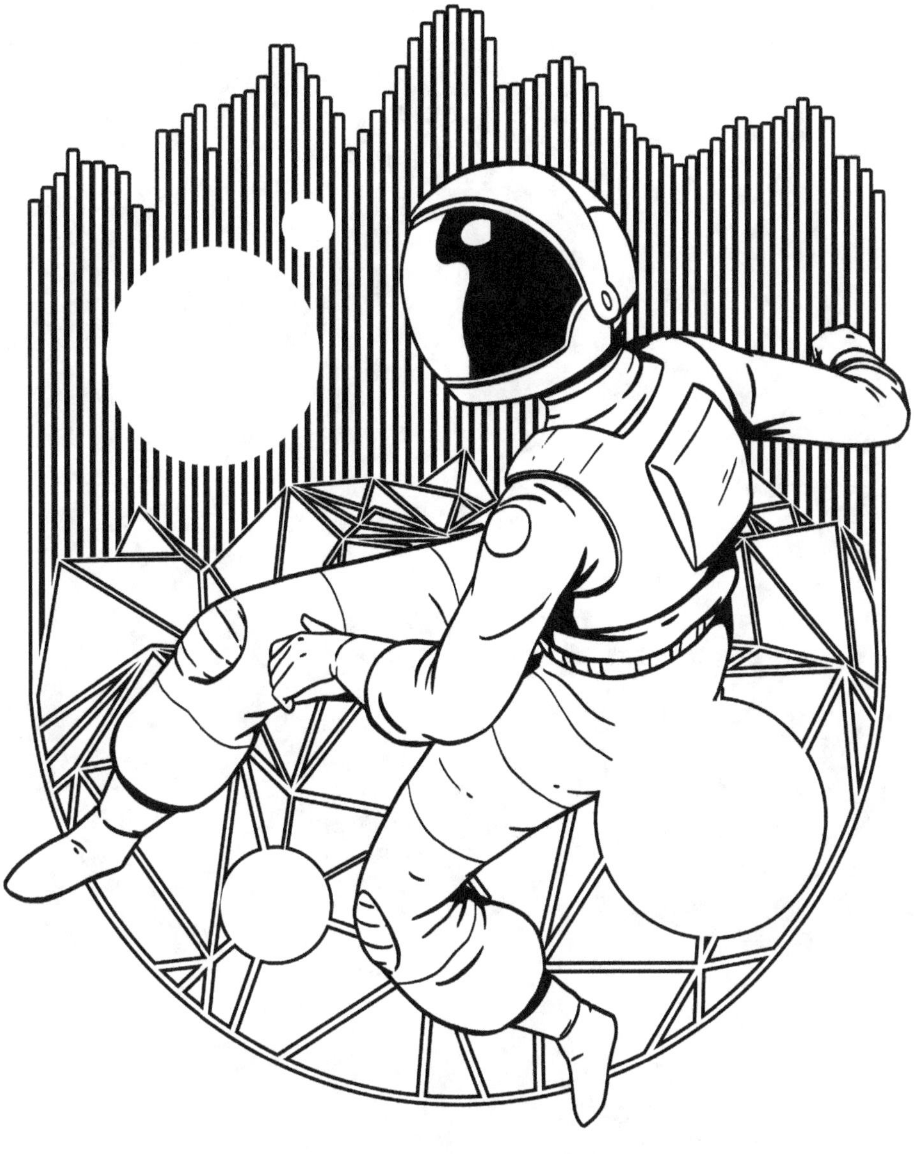

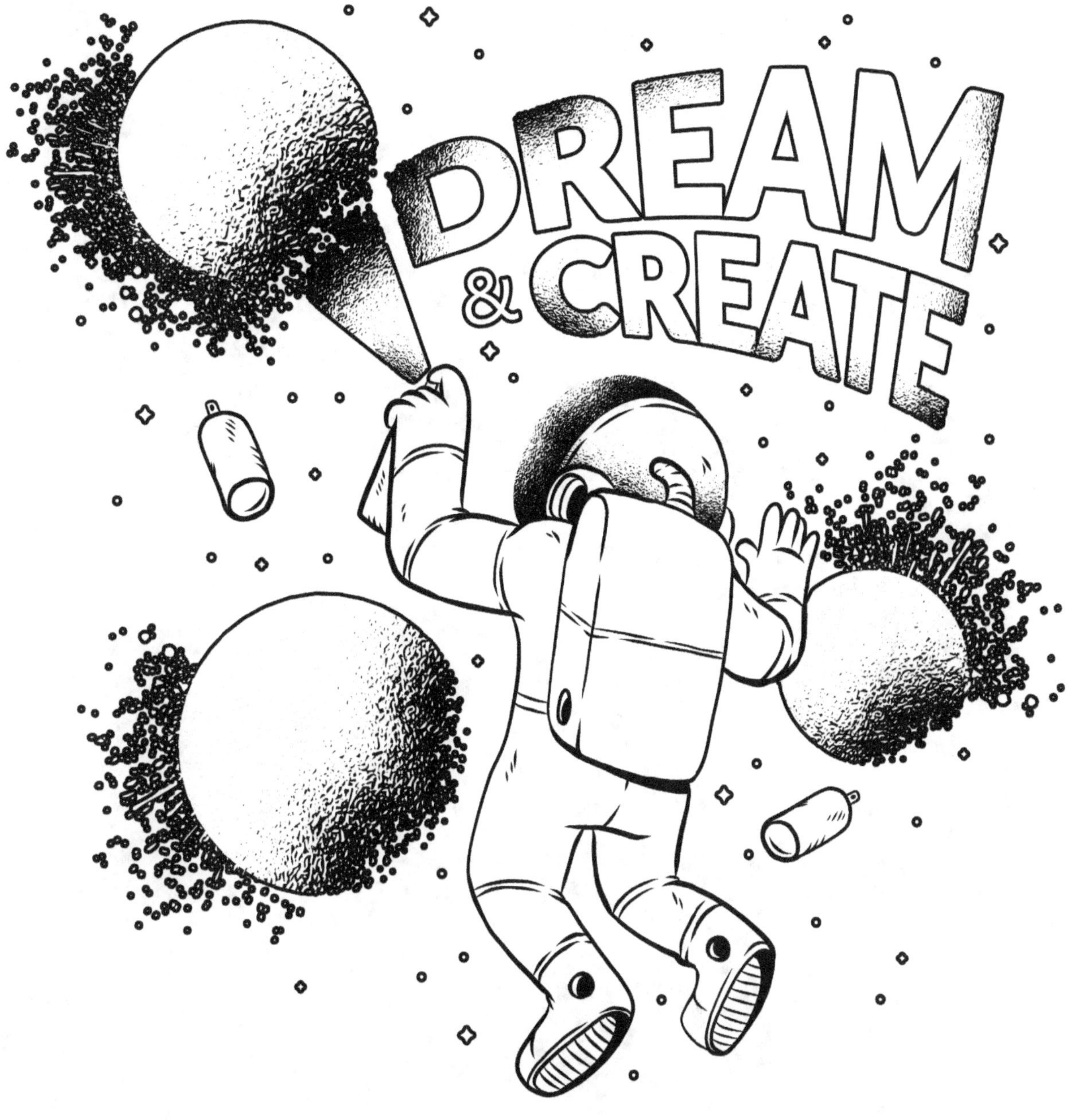
DREAM
& CREATE

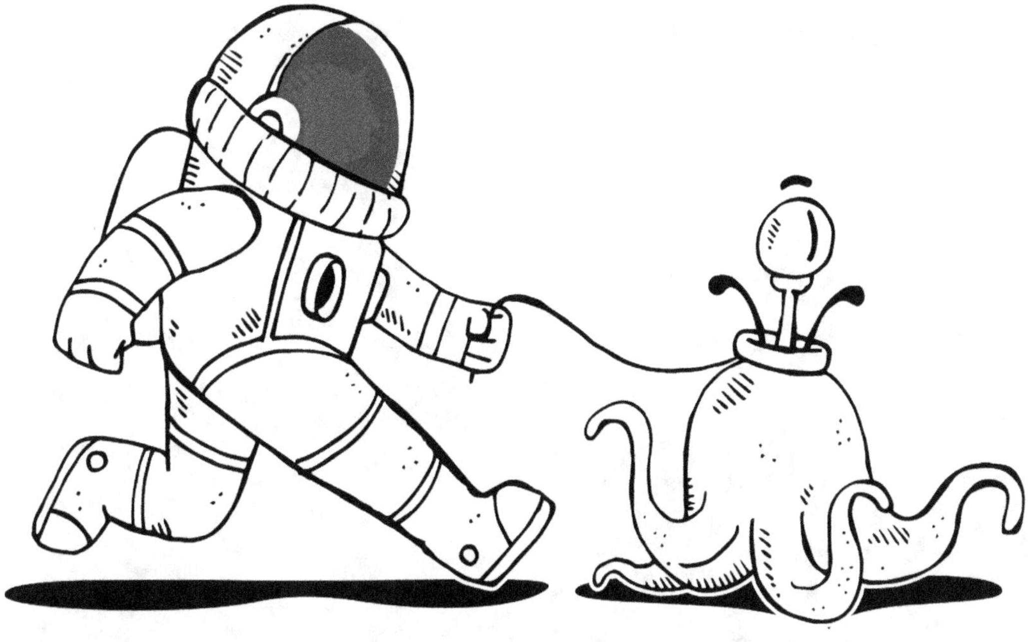

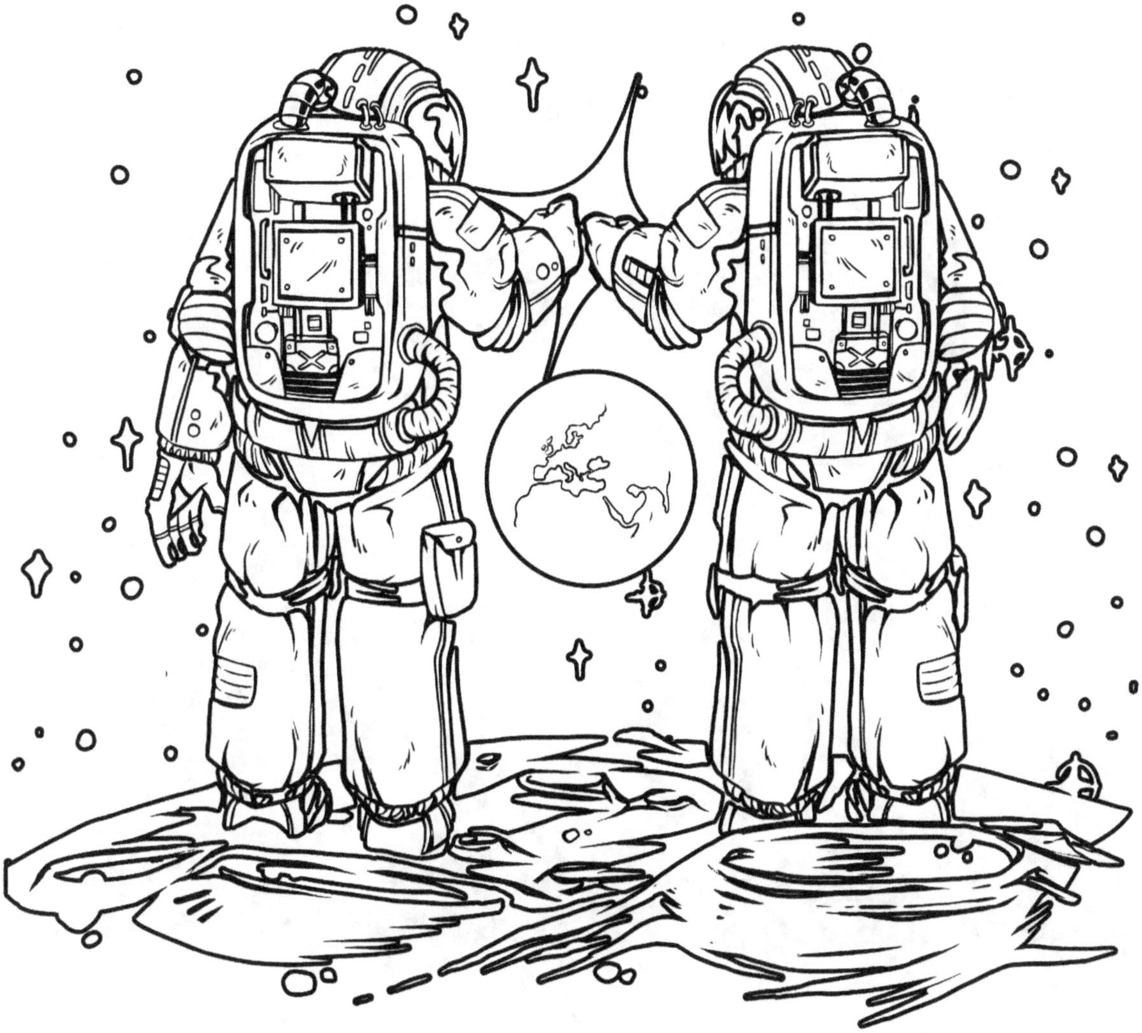

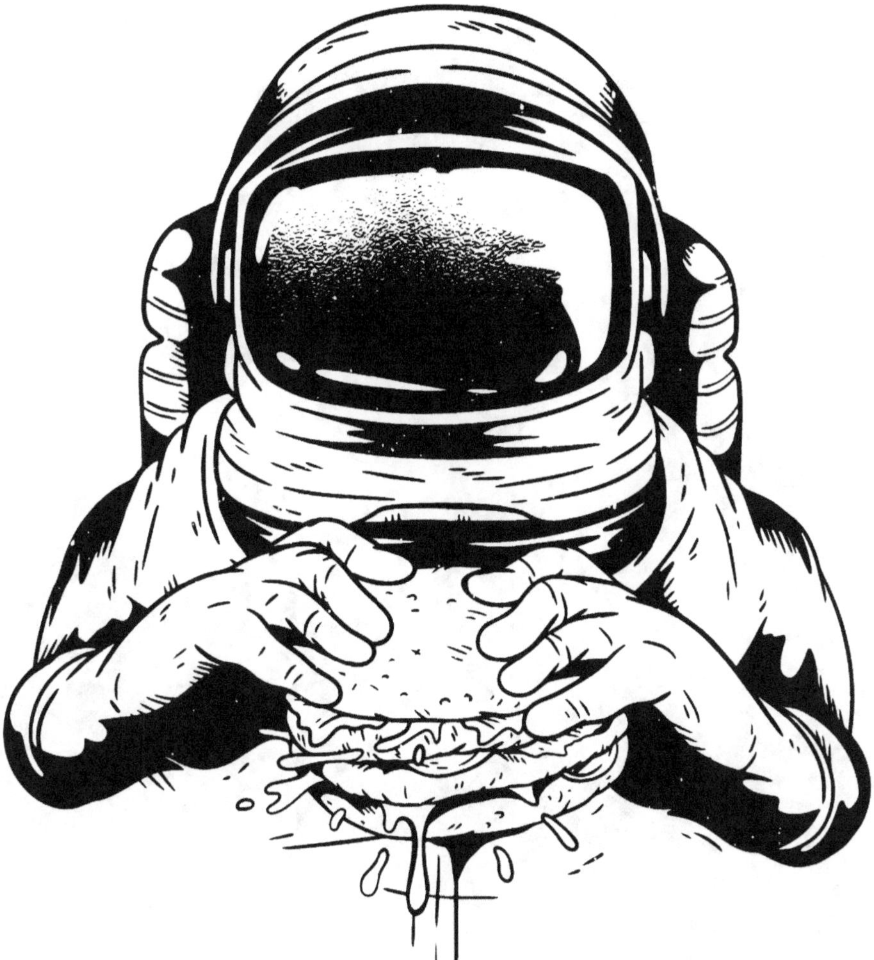

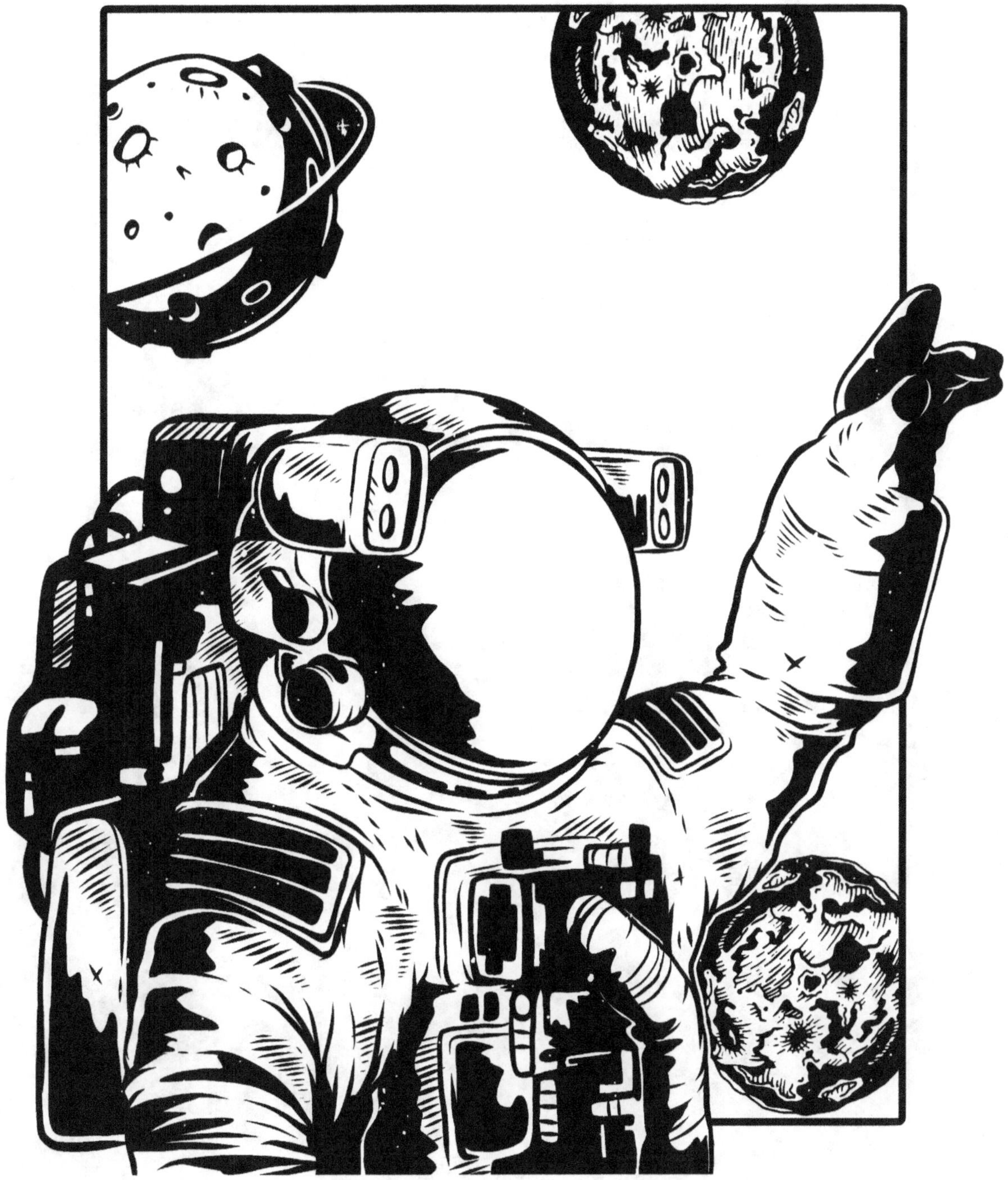

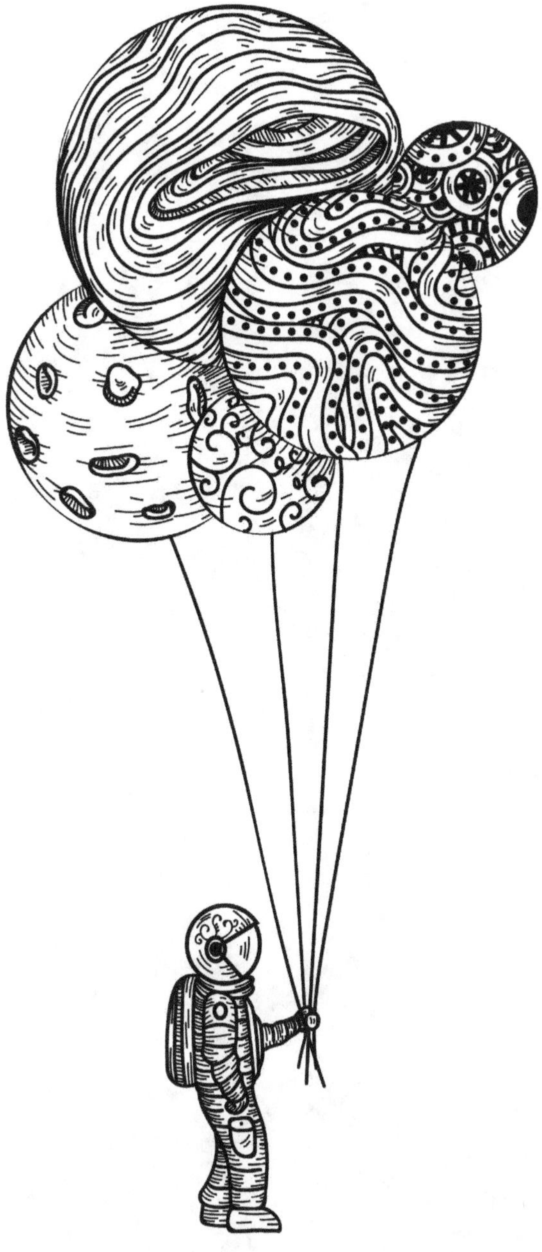

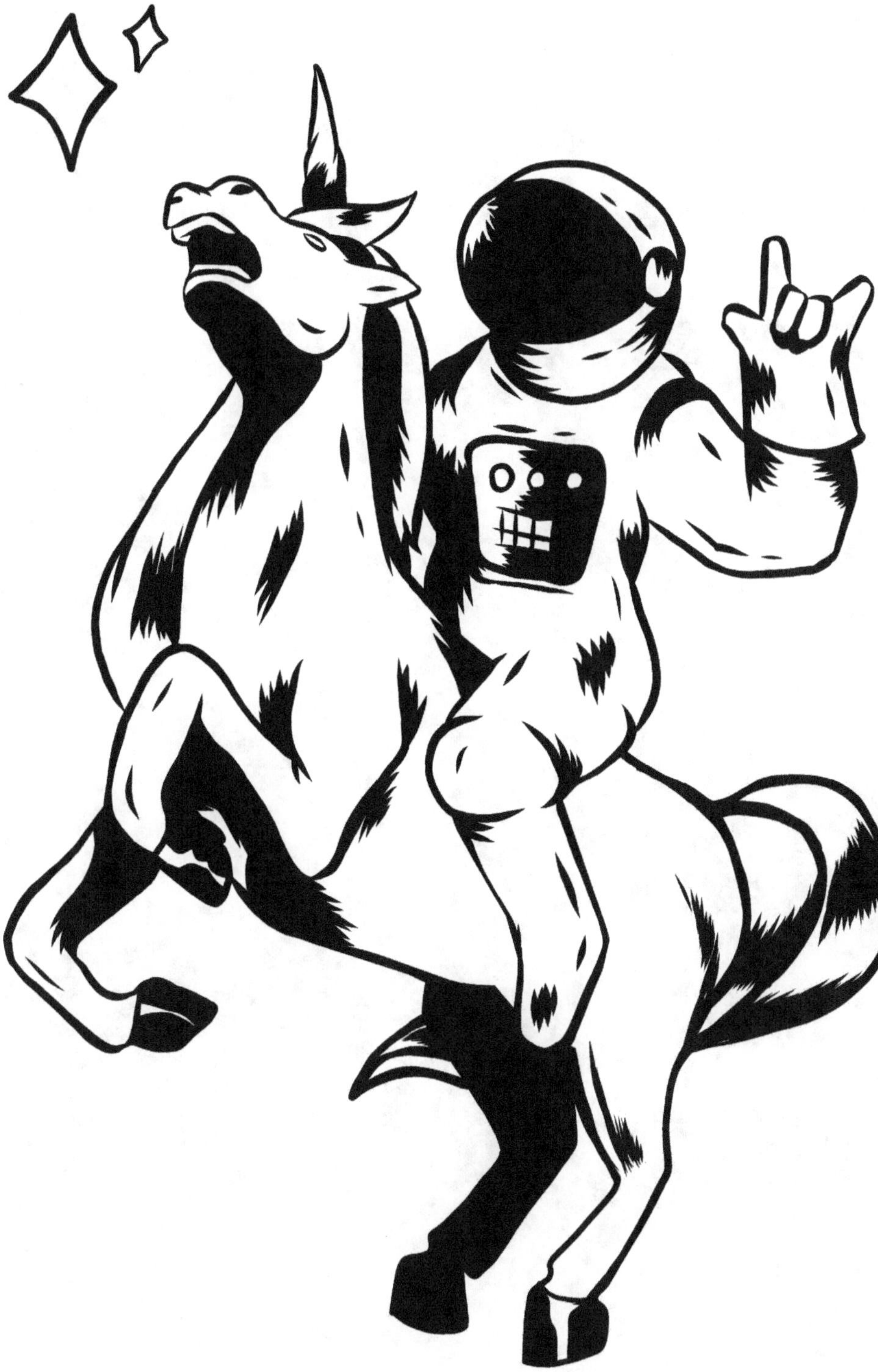

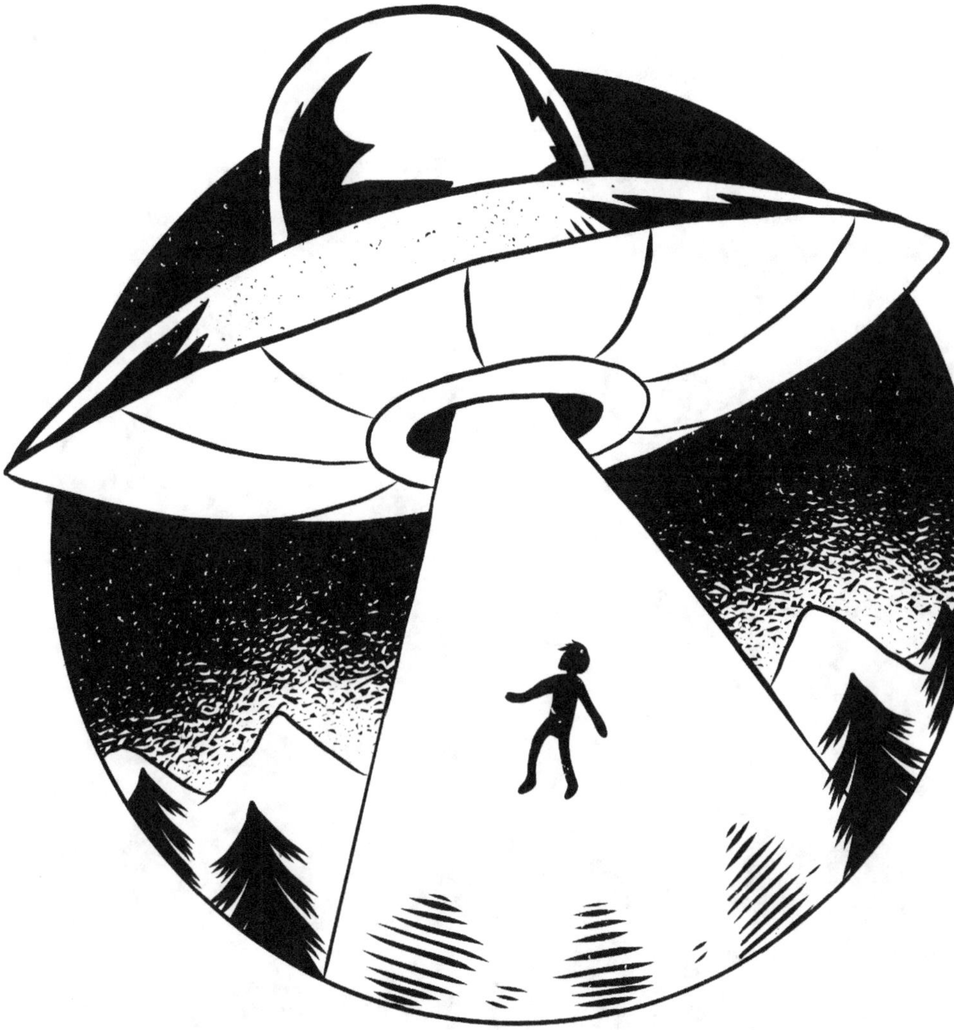

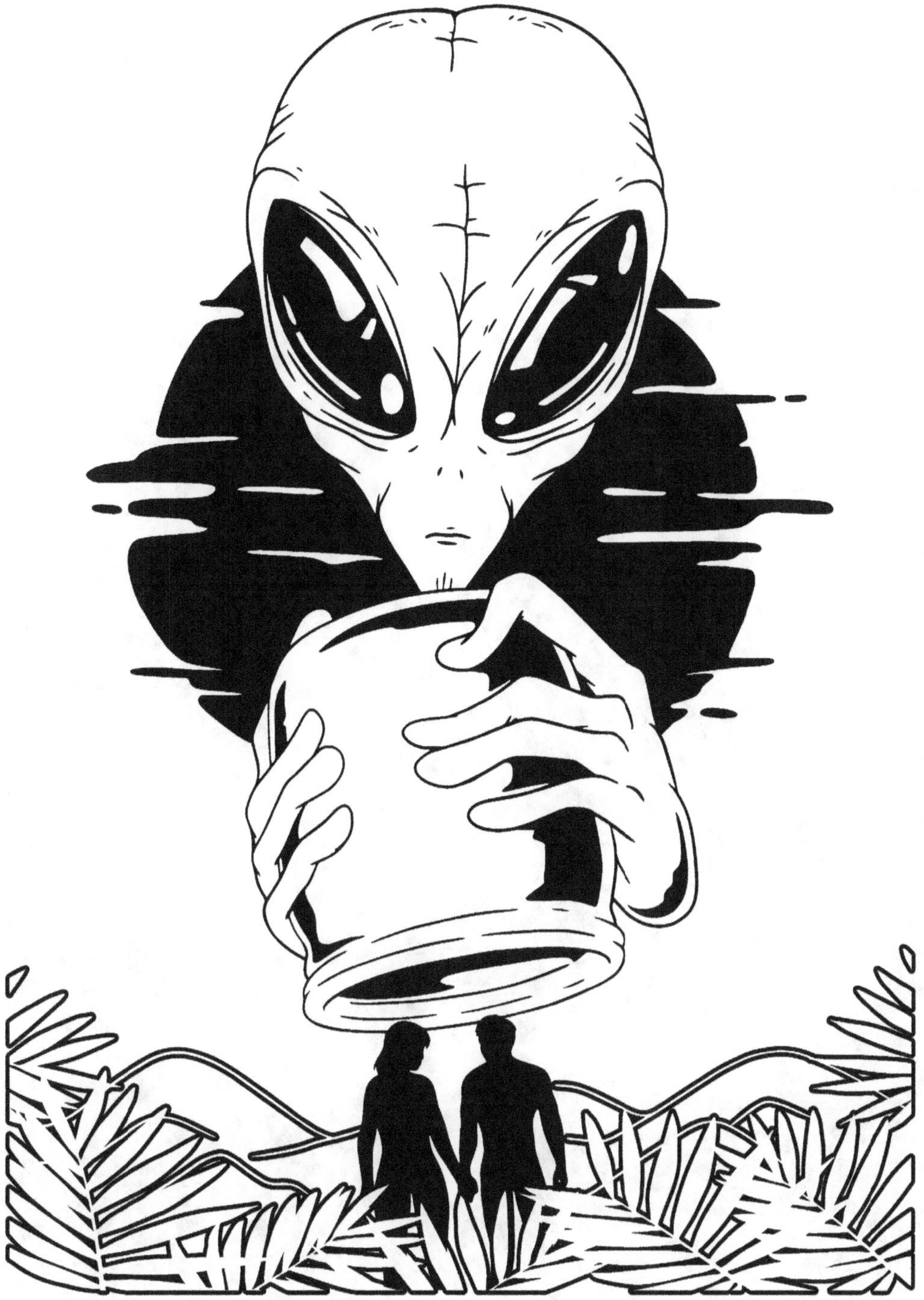

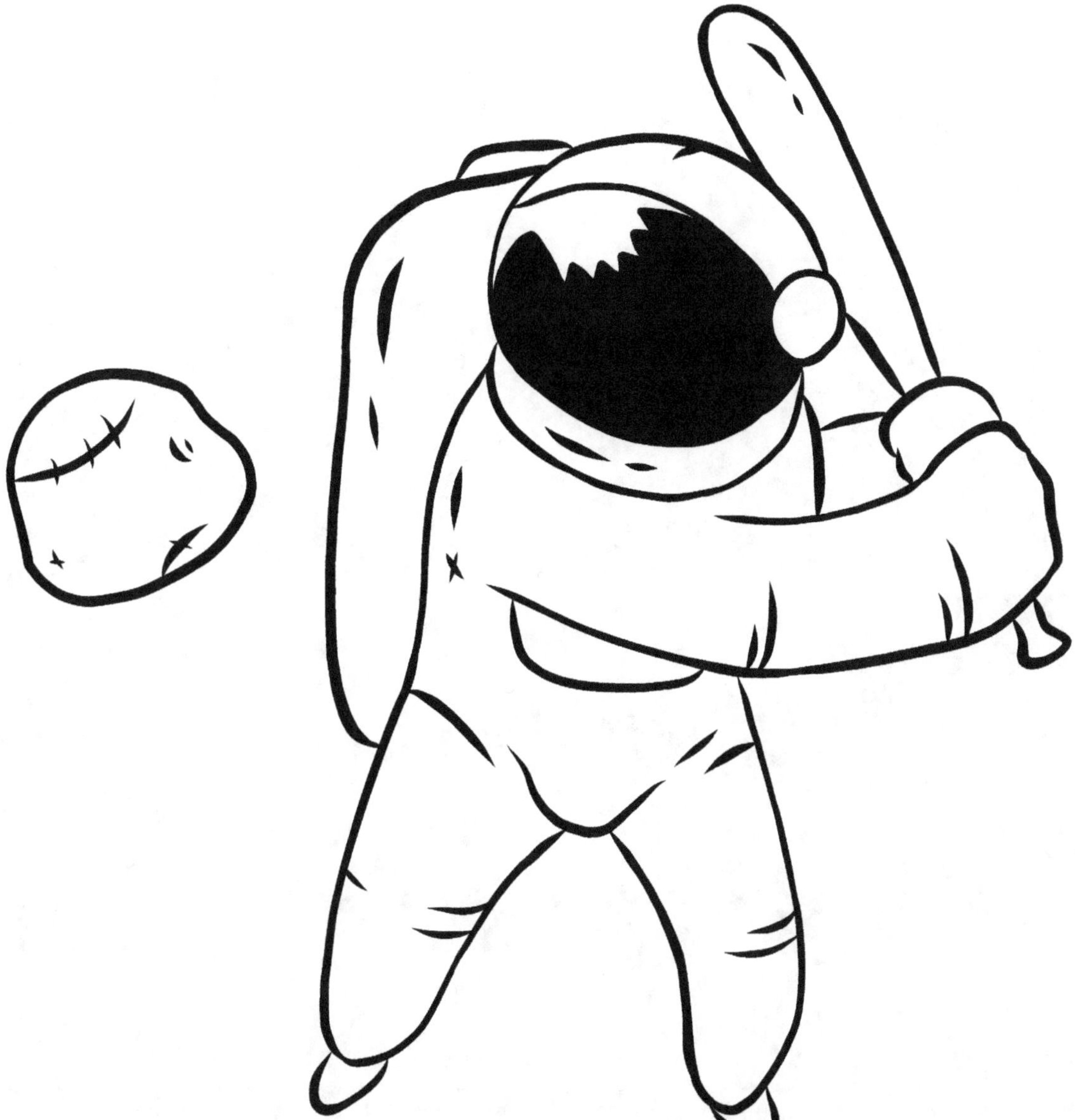

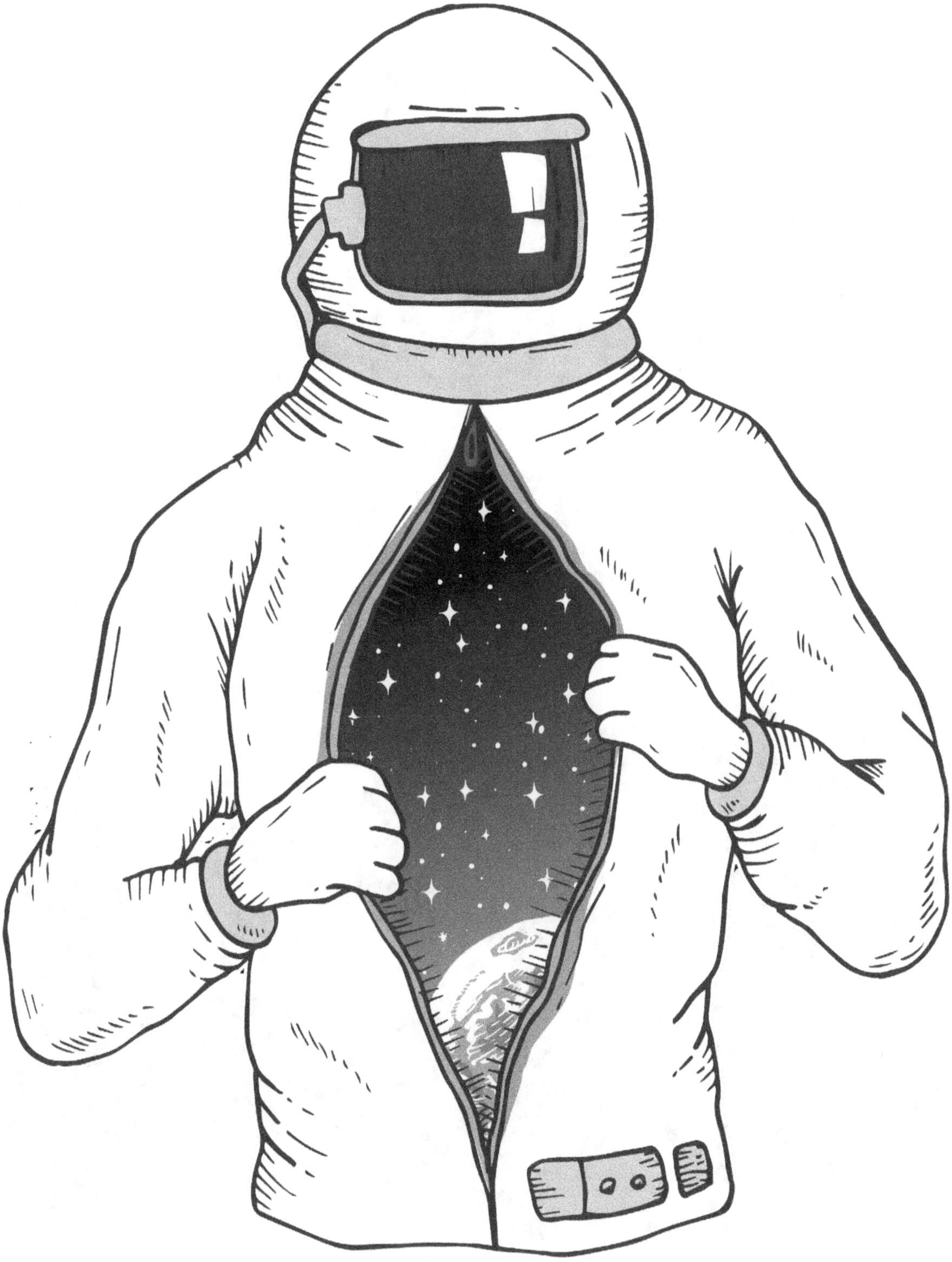

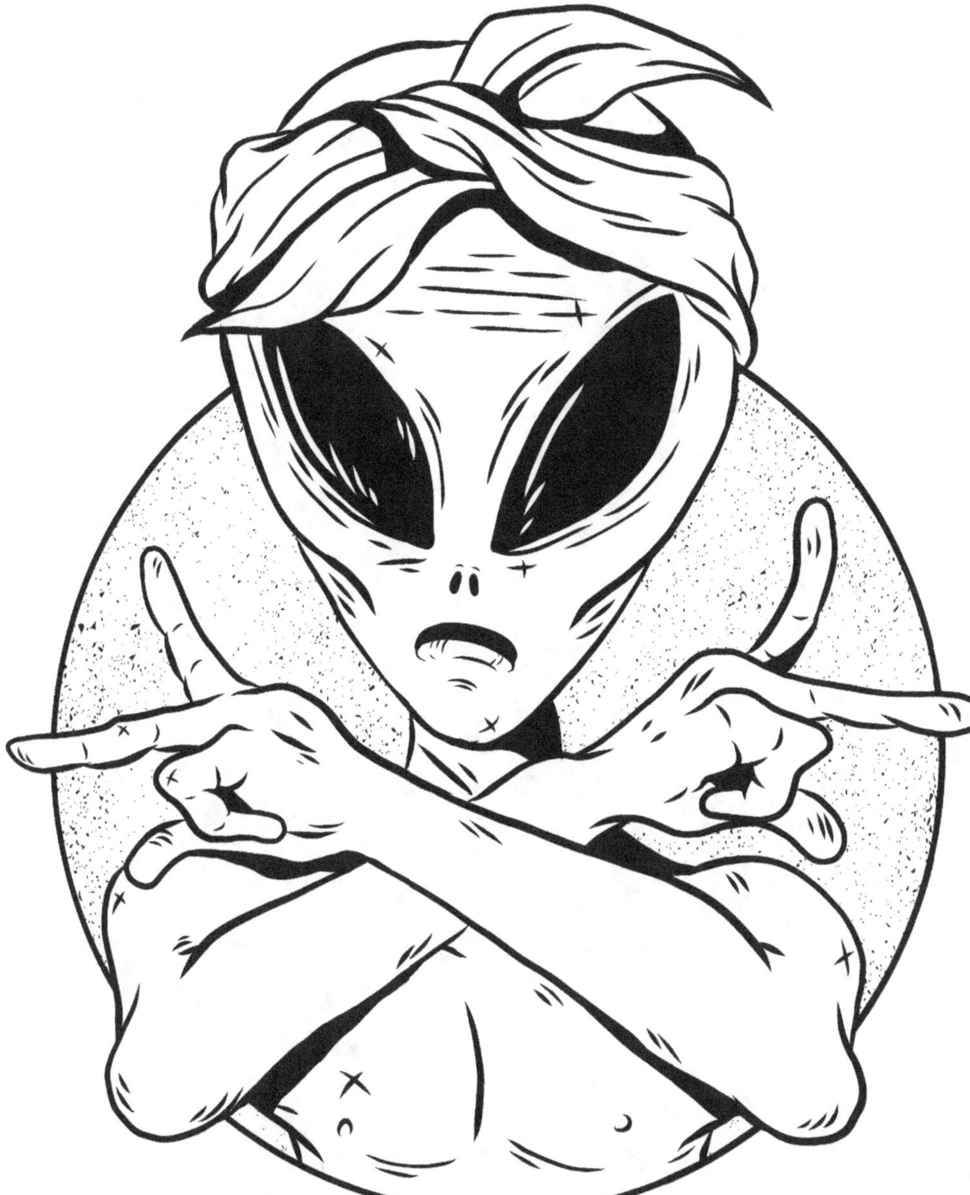

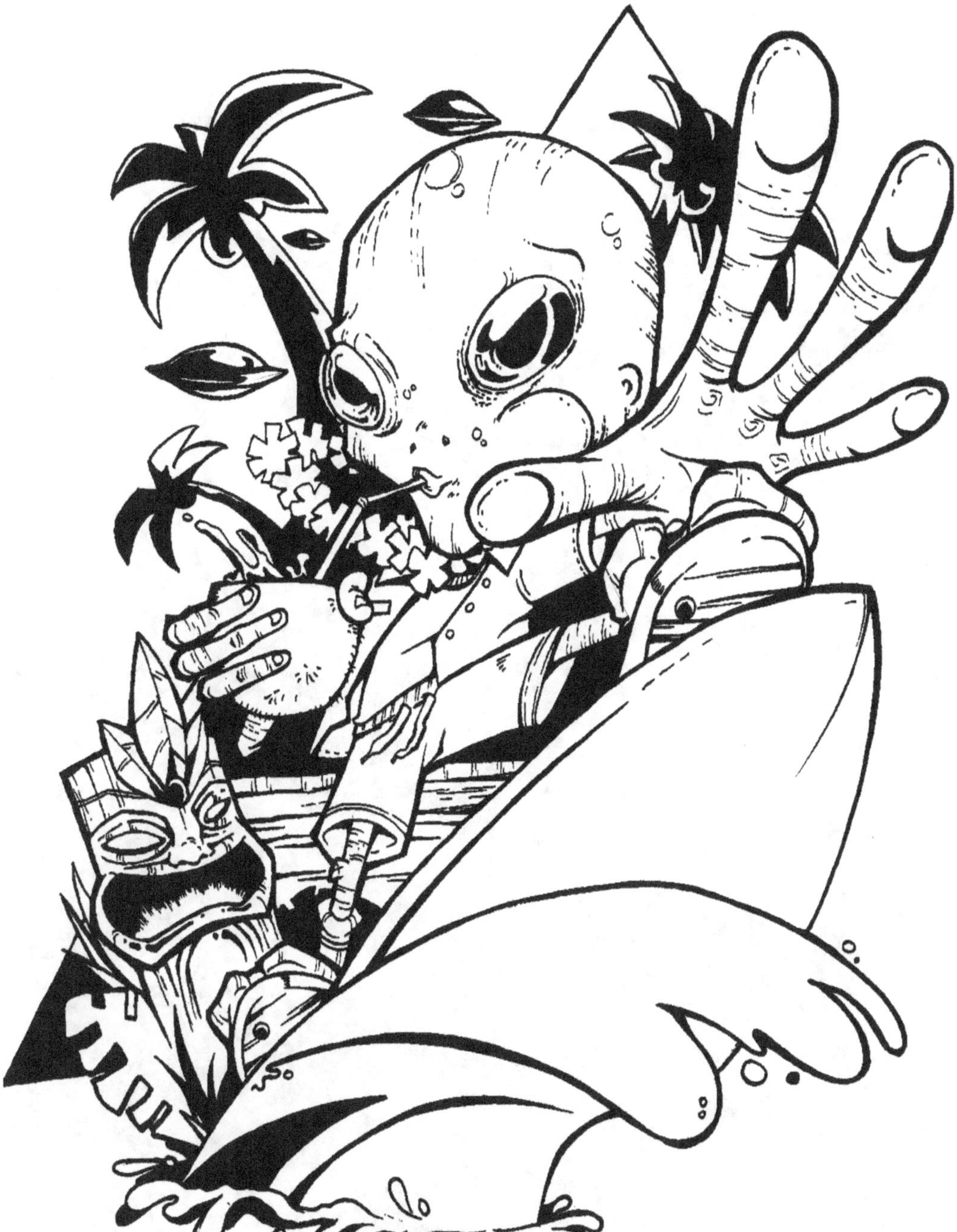

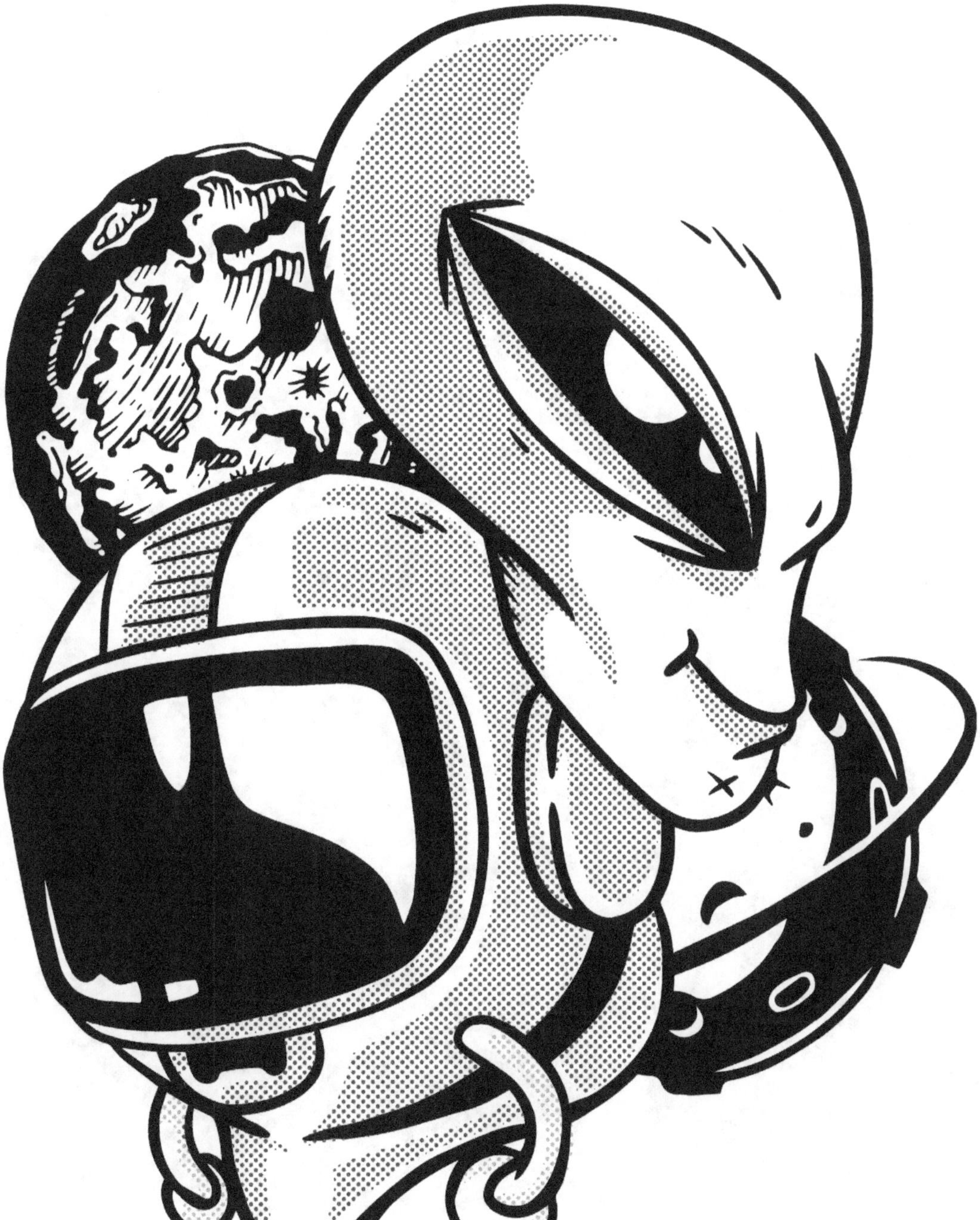

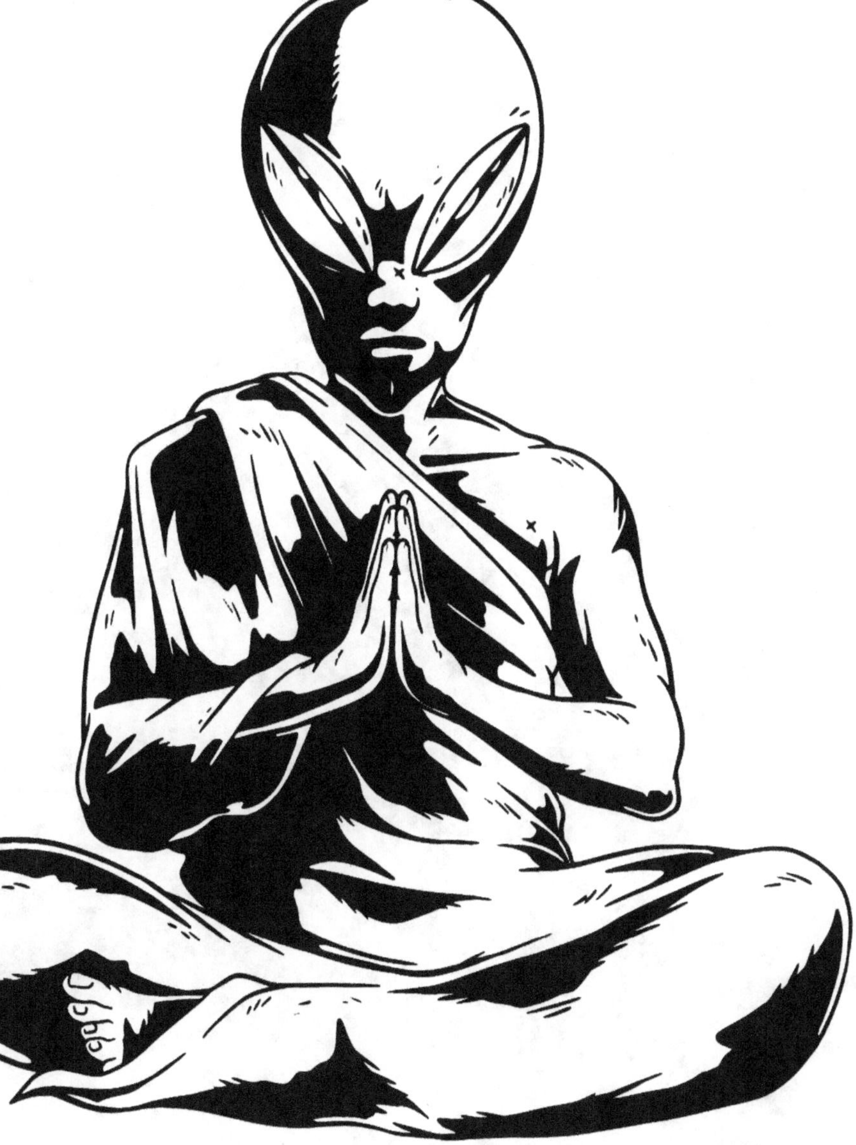

www.ingramcontent.com/pod-product-compliance
Lightning Source LLC
Chambersburg PA
CBHW080905220526
45466CB00011BA/3473